Original title:

Blue Waves, Golden Sun

Copyright © 2025 Creative Arts Management OÜ
All rights reserved.

Author: Juliana Wentworth
ISBN HARDBACK: 978-1-80581-523-5
ISBN PAPERBACK: 978-1-80581-050-6
ISBN EBOOK: 978-1-80581-523-5

The Glistening Line

A seagull stole my sandwich,
With a cheeky little caw.
It swooped right down and snatched it,
Leaving crumbs of pure guffaw.

The kids are building castles,
With moats that have no end.
One toppled in like a jester,
Declaring waves their friend.

Murmurs Beneath the Surface

I pondered what fish whisper,
As they swim and glide away.
Do they gossip about the crab?
Or complain of the sunny day?

A dolphin flipped over, splashing,
Its laughter echoed near.
It said, 'You should try a swim!'
'But I forgot my gear!'

Remnants of Day

The sky painted with orange,
Like a clown in a parade.
I dropped my ice cream cone,
Now it's just a sticky fade.

The sun said, 'Don't be frowning!'
'We'll chase the stars tonight!'
But my wallet sang a tune,
Comedy in the moonlight.

The Kaleidoscope Shore

Footprints dance like silly shapes,
All over the sandy bed.
Some walk straight, others wobbly,
Where did that one clown tread?

A crab wore a tiny sunhat,
To keep its shell from heat.
It strutted like a boss, you see,
Oh, what a funny feat!

Embracing the Day in Turquoise and Apricot

The ocean wears a silly hat,
As crabs dance like they're on a mat.
Seagulls squawk a comical tune,
While sunbeams twirl like a balloon.

Flip-flops squeak in a goofy race,
While jellyfish float with an awkward grace.
Kids build castles that tumble down,
As waves laugh and wear a frothy crown.

A Journey through the Aquamarine and Gleaming Dawn

A fish with glasses swims by with glee,
Sipping on lemonade, so carefree.
A dolphin spins, showing off its flair,
While the sun snores loud and doesn't care.

Turtles in shades take a slow stroll,
Plotting how to sneak a sunbathing goal.
The tide rolls in with a cheeky grin,
Inviting all to jump right in!

Portals of Joy in Luminous Waves.

The sunset splashes paint across the sea,
While a crab parks its ride and grins with glee.
Fish wear bow ties for the evening show,
Prompting all to dance, and away they go!

Waves crack jokes in a bubbly tone,
As dolphins surf on foam like it's their throne.
The horizon spills laughter, bright and loud,
While the sun winks at the gathering crowd.

Eternal Horizon

Waves whisper secrets that tickle the shore,
Playing tag with sandcastle galore.
A seagull juggles shells just for fun,
While the sun draws smiles, never on the run.

The breeze tells tales of a silly dance,
Encouraging turtles to prance and prance.
Sand slips through fingers, laughter in the air,
As time takes a break without a care!

A Tapestry of Light and Currents Untold

The skies are draped in laughter,
While fish put on a show.
They dance amid the bubbles,
In a quest for the deep-fried dough.

With shades of blue and winks of cheer,
Seaweed wigs make waves of fun.
The crabs in tuxedos scuttle near,
As if they've just begun to run.

Warm Embrace of Day and Ocean's Depth

The sun tickles the sandy shore,
While seagulls squawk a tune.
They compete with playful waves galore,
Chasing sunsets 'til the moon.

A dolphin dons a party hat,
Jumps high as laughter fills the breeze.
Each splash is a humorous spat,
Turning fish into avant-garde tease.

Serenading Under the Amber Sky

Beneath the glowing ball of fire,
The jellyfish prepare to prance.
With elegant grace that won't expire,
They wobble into a wiggly dance.

The otters host a wild buffet,
A feast of clams and old old shoes.
Where else would they laugh and play?
In sandcastles, they sing the blues.

A Horizon Glowing in Mélange of Hues

Colors splash, like paint gone wild,
Artists gathered for a spree.
Shells are smiles, laughter compiled,
As crabs argue who's the best at glee.

The day's a jester, funny and bright,
Every wave a tickle, a nudge of cheer.
The coastline whispers, joy takes flight,
With a splash, they disappear in the rear.

Reflections of the Day

Splash and giggle, kids at play,
Chasing crabs that run away.
A seagull steals my sandwich treat,
While I try not to lose my feet.

Buckets flying, hats go soaring,
A dog joins in, it's all exploring.
Sunburned noses, laughter loud,
We're the silliest on the beach, proud.

The Ocean's Lullaby

The tide hums softly, like a cat,
While sea turtles joke and chat.
A crab does the cha-cha near the shore,
While fish wear crowns and beg for more.

Waves break gently, chasing foam,
Seashells gather, make a home.
A dolphin flips, steals the show,
My flip-flops dance, oh what a go!

Horizon's Glow

Sunrise giggles, what a sight,
The sky paints, a colorful light.
Pineapple floats, a fruit parade,
Seashell trumpets, merrily played.

Laughing gulls take flight with flair,
While sunscreen cartoons fill the air.
Sandcastles standing, proud and tall,
This joyous place, we'll never fall.

Sirens of Sunlit Surf

Mermaids sing in flip-flop shoes,
Telling tales of ocean blues.
With hidden treasures, snacks galore,
They splash around, then ask for more.

Shiny fish wear tiny hats,
While seagulls swing like acrobats.
Sandy toes and seaside cheer,
With a wink and a flip, we have no fear.

Tidal Radiance

The ocean giggles with a sway,
Fish wear sunglasses, what a display!
Seagulls dance on breeze so light,
Surfboards wobble, what a sight!

Splashing around, they call it play,
Mermaids hide—no want for delay.
A crab in shorts snips shells galore,
Jellyfish tickle just off the shore.

Praises of the Wind

Whistling tunes with a gusty flair,
It tickles your hair, without a care.
Kites soar high, like they own the sky,
While squirrels giggle as they zip by.

Wind's a prankster, it lifts your hat,
Watch as it teases the chubby cat.
Clouds start a race, they shuffle around,
And trees all dance to a tune profound.

Murmurs of Dawn

Morning's chuckle, the sky's in a suit,
Roosters crow in a wobbly hoot.
Pancakes flip like a circus show,
While toasters jump, quite full of dough.

Sunbeams peek through the curtains wide,
While toast pops up with a hop, a glide.
Coffee's brewing with a giddy cheer,
We laugh at breakfast, the best time of year.

Receding Memories

Footprints wash away with a giggle,
Shells traded for tales that make you wiggle.
A bottle's message from a grumpy fish,
Wants a pizza, oh, what a wish!

Sandcastles crumble, laughter spins,
Kids race the tide, nabbing their wins.
Yet, the sea whispers, "Come visit me,"
Forever chasing that saltwater glee.

Promises of the Dawn

The ocean giggles, a joyful tease,
As seagulls race on the playful breeze.
Sunshine spills like honey on the shore,
While crabs do a dance and the fish humor more.

Shells wear hats, oh what a sight!
Cranky old boats join in on the flight.
Gliding past jellyfish in their fancy jigs,
Splashing about while a dolphin just digs.

The tides pull secrets, they whisper with glee,
"Join us for laughter, come sip on the sea!"
Seagulls squawk tales of their oceanic quests,
While sandcastles giggle in wind's gentle pests.

A sunbeam chuckles, it tickles the waves,
As children splash in their bright little graves.
The day wears a grin, and the sky starts to play,
Every glint in the water says, "Let's frolic today!"

The Horizon's Song

Mr. Sun yawns wide, ready for fun,
While waves wear a hat, all sparkly and done.
Fish put on sunglasses, cool like they are,
Jellyfish groove like they're at a bar.

Seashells gossip, sharing funny tales,
Of turtles who run with the tiniest flails.
Crabs crack jokes, pinching left and right,
While seagulls decide if they'll join in the flight.

The horizon winks, teasing the land,
"Come dance with the sea, it's bold and it's grand!"
The sand tickles toes, a soft, sandy tease,
As waves play hopscotch with the gulls in a breeze.

Night slowly giggles, as stars start to peek,
The ocean's good humor makes everyone speak.
With laughter and joy, let the music resound,
In a world made of fun, where happiness abounds.

Harmonies of Light and Water

In the shimmer of the sea, a fish did dance,
Wearing shades of pink, it sought romance.
A seagull squawked as if to say,
"Stop your wiggles, it's a judgment day!"

Fluffy clouds drifted like ice cream swirls,
While turtles debated over fancy pearls.
The crab tapped his toes to the ocean's beat,
Claiming he was the king of the salty sheet.

Surfers attempting to ride the breeze,
Fell off their boards with practiced ease.
The ocean giggled, splashing with glee,
"Who knew riding waves would cost a fee?"

Laughter erupted as all gathered 'round,
For each wave carried a new silly sound.
In the sun's warmth, they danced and played,
Creating memories that would never fade.

The Sunkissed Odyssey

Upon the shore, they sang a tune,
While bathed in light beneath the moon.
A beach ball bounced and smacked a crab,
With a flip and a flap, he found quite a fab!

As flip-flops flew and shells got piled,
The beachgoers chortled with humor wild.
Caught in a net, a fish made a bid,
"Let me out, I'm no mermaid's kid!"

Seagulls swooped, attending the feast,
Stealing hot fries from the hungry beast.
With ketchup in hand, a little child screamed,
"Oh no, my snack! How did you scheme?"

The sun was setting, colors ablaze,
As laughter rang out in a sunset haze.
Buffoons of the beach, what a delightful mirth,
A memorable day, the best of their worth!

A Cascade of Colors

In the ocean's cradle, hues collide,
Where fishes giggle, and dolphins slide.
A clam cracked jokes with a glittery pearl,
"You'll be late for the bash if you don't twirl!"

Each shell wore colors like crazy hats,
While crabs held parties, inviting the chats.
The jellyfish floated, a blobby balloon,
"I'm an artist! Give me a whacky tune!"

The sun splashed gold like a painter's hand,
Creating a canvas so vibrant and grand.
While stripes of joy splattered all around,
Even the seaweed was dancing unbound!

From tidal pools, giggles burst to the air,
In this funny kingdom with laughter to spare.
Together they swayed, a delightful brigade,
Painting the beach, a memory made!

Illuminated Journeys

Beneath glittering hues, they set on a spree,
With umbrellas and flip-flops, a wacky jubilee.
Each step on the sand led to quirky sights,
Like the sunny piñata with silly insights.

The beach towels flapped with comedic flair,
As playful waves chased without a care.
They built castles that fell with a splash,
A royal decree of a hilarious crash!

Seagulls argued over who gets the fry,
While beachgoers stumbled and laughed at the sky.
With every toppled scoop of ice-cream mess,
The day dripped laughter, their joys to confess.

In the glow of twilight, their spirits soared,
Embracing the quirks that life had stored.
With shoulders shaking, they danced on the shore,
Creating a tale they'd cherish and adore.

Mirage of the Sea

In a land where fish wear hats,
And seagulls dance like acrobats,
The ocean sings a silly tune,
As crabs breakdance beneath the moon.

A dolphin pranks a passing boat,
While mermaids giggle, then they gloat.
A seaweed war for hullabaloo,
The underwater circus comes into view.

With flamingos painted neon bright,
They splashed around, oh what a sight!
The waves were filled with laughter's roar,
As jellyfish played like never before.

So come and join this wild parade,
For silly antics never fade.
Let's toast with shells, a drink so grand,
In this mirage of our frothy land.

Whispers of Liquid Gold

In puddles glittering like prize games,
The fish audition for TV fame.
Octopuses weave their fashion styles,
Their outfits making everyone smile.

A crab sings karaoke at dusk,
While seashells dance, with nary a fuss.
Jellybeans wash up on the shore,
As the clams tell jokes, we beg for more.

With a pinch of salt and a squeeze of lime,
The waves all chuckle, it's joke time!
The sandcastles joke, they're never too tall,
A funny twist, they still have a ball.

So let the splash and giggles unfold,
In whispers bright, like liquid gold.
With laughter shared among the sea crew,
Every wave has a punchline too!

Sweet Caress of the Tide

The tide rolls in with a playful grin,
While starfish practice violin.
The air is filled with silly cheers,
As splashing crabs lose count of years.

Seashells hold a gossip fest,
With sea turtles showing off their best.
A whale's got puns to share with the crowd,
As fish go surfing, feeling proud.

Paddleboards shaped like giant pies,
Catch seagulls trying to surf the skies.
With every wave, a giggle hides,
In this sweet mess where laughter glides.

So let the waters tickle your toes,
As the happy tide merrily flows.
In every splash, a new joke rides,
With the jokes as bright as the water slides!

Saffron Skies

As dawn breaks with colors so wild,
The turtles dance, like cheeky children smiled.
They paint the clouds with cotton candy,
Whisking gusts, oh so dandy!

Seagulls practice their comedic acts,
While crabs trade gossip, no time for slacks.
An octopus attempts to do a jig,
But slips on slime—it's all quite big!

With flamingos wearing shades of pink,
They joke about the ocean's stink.
Tail-feathered friends, they laugh and cheer,
As the sun peeks in, bright and near.

So bask beneath the saffron hue,
Where every twist bounces and renews.
In this cheeky glow where fun resides,
We dance with the tides, with silly strides!

Sunlit Currents

Splashing laughter in the tide,
Seagulls waltz, side by side.
Tanned otters, snoozing fast,
Dreaming of their surfboard cast.

Crabs wear shades, looking cool,
Dancing under sunbeam rule.
Starfish gossip, tales to tell,
While clam shells giggle, oh so well.

Waves come crashing, oh what fun,
Turtlenecks on, we're not done!
Sandy toes and sunscreen eyes,
Building castles as time flies.

At the end, we take a dip,
Water's chilly – who will skip?
Floating jokes through salty foam,
Here's to fun, we're all at home!

Echoes of the Distant Shore

Whales make calls that sound like cheers,
Shells collect our giggling tears.
Cranky crabs, with tiny grins,
Racing waves like they're on twins.

Breezy hats fly off with flair,
Caught by dolphins unaware.
Beach ball bounces, laughter soars,
Sunburnt noses risk applause.

Sandcastles with moats like dreams,
Where jellybeans flow in streams.
Each wave whispers a silly joke,
As seashells join in with a poke.

The sky's a blanket, crayon blue,
As we burrow, just me and you.
Tickling toes, the sea hugs tight,
In this giggle fest of delight!

Celestial Ripples

Starfish dance in cosmic glow,
Jellyfish in tutu flow.
Giggling waves that tickle feet,
Join the jolly, joyous beat.

Sandy sculptures, kings of jest,
Sandpipers squawking, doing best.
The ocean hums a silly tune,
While the sun dons its shiny croon.

Each splash is laughter, rolling wide,
With beachy jokes left open wide.
Seashells chuckle, secrets shared,
In ocean's choir, no one's spared.

Under the sun, what a sight!
Fish wear glasses, feeling bright.
Together we'll jump, dive, and spin,
In this honking fun we're in!

Golden Embrace on the Shore

Kites zoom high, they try to soar,
As flip-flops fly from store to store.
Sandwiches stick like silly glue,
When a hungry seagull swoops on through!

Flip-flops squeak on the warm sand,
Giggling kids wave their hands.
Bunnies hop, doing the jig,
Seeking a snack, what a big gig!

Buckets filled with mismatched toys,
Frolicking 'round, filled with joys.
A sand crab wears a party hat,
While we laugh and dance on the mat.

As the sun sinks low and bright,
Shadows stretch into the night.
Together we'll leave with a cheer,
Sandy hearts, we'll hold dear!

Ripple of Gold

The ocean giggles, full of cheer,
As sandy toes dance without fear.
Seagulls squawk, a comedic show,
While sun hats fly, oh no, oh no!

Splashing friends with water balloons,
Laughing hard like silly loons.
A crab in shades struts on the shore,
Claiming it's king, we all want more!

With sunscreen battles, oh what a sight!
We smear it on, yet still we fight.
A jellyfish wears a prince's crown,
Who knew the sea was such a clown?

As sunsets blush, we end the day,
With laughter ringing, come what may.
The ripple of joy, it won't decay,
In our hearts, forever to stay.

Kiss of the Surf

The tide rolls in with a playful kiss,
Splashing our worries, pure bliss!
Flip-flops fly like they have wings,
While seagulls steal our tasty things!

With sunscreen smudged on all our noses,
We dance like we've got garden hoses.
A wave crashes, we tumble in,
As laughter bubbles, let the fun begin!

Surfboards wobble, oh what a ride,
We squeal and giggle, caught by the tide.
Beach balls bouncing, a game of chase,
The ocean's grin can't be replaced!

As the sun dips low and shadows grow,
We find seashells in the golden glow.
A day well spent, with joy so bright,
We dream of surf and moonlit night.

The Shimmering Edge

At the water's edge, the shimmer calls,
Where laughter rises, and no one stalls.
A hermit crab plays hide and seek,
In his tiny shell, he's quite unique!

Our beach party is a wacky scene,
With fruity drinks and sunscreen sheen.
A sandcastle stands, oh what a feat,
With towers that wobble beneath our feet!

We race the tide, who's faster still?
Sandy giants give us a thrill.
A dolphin dives with a cheeky grin,
As seagulls shout, "Let the games begin!"

As golden hour paints the sky,
We watch the sunset, oh my, oh my!
The shimmering waves hold stories unfurled,
In our hearts, a magical world.

Horizon's Lullaby

The horizon hums a silly tune,
As cheeky waves and giggling dunes.
Seashells sing as they join the fun,
While kids chase crabs under the sun!

We build epic forts with driftwood and glee,
As tides tiptoe in, a playful spree.
A dolphin leaps with an acrobatic flair,
While we all cheer, "Look, over there!"

The sand is now our wiggly throne,
Where laughter echoes and we've never grown.
Snow cones dribble, sweet treats galore,
Life's a beach, who could ask for more?

As dusk arrives, the stars will play,
While moonlit waves twinkle and sway.
Horizon's lullaby, soft and bright,
In our dreams, we'll surf through the night.

Mermaids' Serenade

Bubbles rise with giggles bright,
Fish all dance in pure delight.
Tails a-splash, they spin around,
In the sea, their joy is found.

Seahorses wear their finest gowns,
Clownfish joke and swim in crowns.
Shells and pearls make quite a scene,
Mermaids wave, what could be green?

A starfish plays the ukulele,
Sings of snacks like jelly jelly.
Break the waves with laughter loud,
The ocean floor, a silly crowd!

Together they make quite the noise,
Silly games and joyful boys.
Underwater, fun won't cease,
Life is wacky, life is peace.

Embrace of the Twilight

The sky's a canvas, what a sight!
Crabs are dancing, feeling right.
Stars peek out from inky blue,
While sea cucumbers sing too!

Shadows stretch and sea dogs bark,
Fish in tuxedos make their mark.
Moonlight glimmers on the sand,
As octopuses form a band.

They strum on guitars made of shells,
While jellyfish spread funny yell-s.
Their bioluminescence glows,
As laughter in the ocean flows.

Seahorses ride the waves with flair,
Twilight charms, a joyful air.
Tonight's the night for underwater cheer,
When friends swim close and play all year!

Illumination of the Deep

Down below where sunlight peeks,
Fish in hats giggle, play hide and seek.
Coral castles all glow in glee,
As squids do their dance, oh look at me!

The anglerfish throws a rave,
With disco lights that surely brave.
Blowfish puff and puff 'til bright,
Their spiky parties, quite the sight!

Crabs roll in with ticklish feet,
In a conga line, oh what a feat!
They twirl and whirl, so full of zest,
Down in the deep, it's a hilarious fest!

With plankton glow in shades of green,
The dance floor shines, a sparkling scene.
Underwater friends burst forth with cheer,
In this bright realm, there's nothing to fear!

The Gilded Dream

Surfers laugh on candy shores,
Wipeouts net them silly scores.
Seashells whisper tales of gold,
With legends bright that never get old.

Dolphins leap in joyous arcs,
While seagulls squawk with bustling sparks.
A treasure map! But wait, oh no!
It leads to picnic spots, let's go!

Cramped on dinner plates they delve,
As crabs parade and shrimp disperse.
They feast on sand and salty fries,
With ocean breeze spun through the skies!

In the midst of giggles and cheer,
Every sunset brings smiles near.
Here's to laughter, fun, and schemes,
Drifting along in gilded dreams!

Celestial Melodies and Ocean's Hues

The sky wore shades of silly glee,
While fish sang songs of jubilee.
A crab danced with a quirky charm,
Waving its claws, oh so disarm!

Seagulls giggled, swooping low,
As dolphins put on quite a show.
A beach ball bounced like a playful pup,
While the sand chased all the waves up!

In costumes bright, the sunbeams pranced,
While jellyfish swayed, quite entranced.
Each ray a wink, a laughter shared,
In colors wild, the world was dared!

So let us dance upon the shore,
With ocean's laughter, we'll adore.
A melody of joy and fun,
As day gives way, the night's begun!

A Symphony of Radiance and Deep Waters

The ocean sparked with goofy smiles,
As clownfish swam in silly styles.
A sea turtle wore a party hat,
While starfish giggled, "What of that?"

With bubbles bursting like balloons,
The lobsters played some catchy tunes.
An octopus tapped its many feet,
Creating rhythms oh so sweet!

A frolicsome breeze began to tease,
While sea foam danced with the golden ease.
Each splash a trick, a playful jest,
The joyous waves put fun to the test!

So let us sing with voice so clear,
As the kooky sea creatures cheer.
In this bright world of laughter spun,
The ocean's ball has just begun!

Nauplius of Gold in the Indigo Sea

A nauplius strutted in pure delight,
Wearing sunglasses so shiny and bright.
With tiny boots, it took to the floor,
Saying, "Watch me dance! Who could want more?"

In laughter-filled schools, the fish did glide,
With jokes so fishy they just couldn't hide.
A parrotfish said, "What's the deal?
When sharks are about, let's keep it real!"

Beneath the waves, the fun flowed fast,
While mischievous crabs played the cast.
Each ripple echoed giggles galore,
As the sun dropped low, we begged for more!

From coral reefs, the ruckus arose,
As the ocean's heart beguiled in prose.
In hues of laughter, the tale is spun,
Of a clever nauplius having fun!

Luminescent Moments at Daybreak

As dawn broke out with a cheeky grin,
The sea greeted us like a playful kin.
With wiggly rays and a splash of cheer,
The ocean's giggles we could hear!

A seahorse in polka dots took flight,
Doing the twist with all its might.
Crabs in sunglasses posed on the sand,
Saying, "Join us now, it's really grand!"

The morning light painted with flair,
Tickling toes in the salty air.
With laughter bubbling in every shell,
The seashells whispered, "Can't you tell?"

As the sun yawned wide, the fun began,
With ocean stories of each little clam.
From dawn till dusk, let joy unfurl,
In this silly sea, we'll dance and swirl!

A Symphony in Azure

In a sea of laughter, fish dance to a tune,
Seagulls sing high, they're quite the buffoons.
Crabs wearing sunglasses, they strut on the shore,
While a jellyfish jiggles and begs for encore.

Turtle on a surfboard, gives quite the show,
Waves tickle his toes, as he rides to and fro.
Flip-flops are flapping, a stylish parade,
Even the starfish have come out to play.

The lifeguard is snoring, a sunburned bright red,
While kids build their castles, and dreams in their head.
The wind whispers secrets to shells in the sand,
As the sun starts to giggle, it's a sight oh so grand.

With laughter and joy, we dance with the tide,
Every splash is a joke in this wild sunny ride.
We wave to the horizon, jointly we jest,
In this vibrant, silly, seaside fest.

Glistening Reflections

Splashes of laughter, under the sun's grin,
Fish wear their tuxedos, waiting to win.
A dolphin deep dives, comes up with a wink,
Splashing all around, it gives everyone a blink.

The lifeguard's on break, sipping on a float,
While a kid on a noodle tries hard not to gloat.
Seagulls run wild, stealing chips from the pack,
While a crab in the corner is planning his snack.

Shadows stretch long, as the sun makes its pitch,
Ice creams are melting, oh what a sweet glitch!
With giggles and splashes, let the fun never stop,
On this mirror of joy, we'll laugh till we drop.

Here on this coastline, life sparkles and twirls,
Every heart beats to the rhythm, each laugh unfurls.
As the tide comes and goes, we'll dance in delight,
With friends by our side, everything feels right.

The Radiant Embrace

A cloud swings by with a sassy little grin,
While the sun throws confetti, shining from within.
A dog leaps with joy, chasing waves that retreat,
While a small child squeals, dancing on sandy feet.

Ocean's a prankster, it tickles our toes,
Bubbles tick-tock, like a clock that just glows.
A sunscreen battle erupts, with splats and with fun,
As umbrellas twirl like they're out on the run.

The tide rolls in softly, but the laughter erupts,
Shells join the chorus, the happy mix-ups.
With ice cream in hand and a monkey in sight,
Every moment we cherish, all feels so right.

In this joyful embrace, let the good times roll,
With sunshine and giggles that tickle the soul.
As day turns to dusk, with a wink in the air,
We'll cherish these moments, a joyful affair.

Azure Dreams

Flip-flops are flying, like birds on a spree,
While fish play charades, just for you and me.
The waves tell a story, all shimmering and bright,
As laughter erupts in the golden sunlight.

A seagull takes selfies, with a crab in its claw,
The kids launch a rocket made of driftwood and straw.
With every small splash, giggles fill the air,
As sunscreen battles rage with no signs of care.

Sun hats and giggles collide in delight,
Footprints are scribbled, oh what a sight!
With hearts full of joy, we make silly poses,
While ocean waves crash like a box of pink roses.

With laughter contagious, the day starts to fade,
We dance like the waves, in this moment we've made.
As the stars poke their heads, reminders that gleam,
We'll treasure these times, in our wild, sunny dream.

A Palette of Serenity

On sandy shores where laughter's found,
Seagulls dive with silly sounds.
The chilly breeze tickles our toes,
As we chase crabs in ludicrous rows.

A piña colada, a splash too high,
A coconut hat flies off to the sky.
We giggle at each splashing dive,
Wishing mermaids were slightly alive.

The sun's a big, bright, glowing ball,
Playing peek-a-boo above us all.
Beneath its rays, we dance and sway,
Turning sunscreen into our ballet.

With sand in our hair, we pose like stars,
Building castles with cookie jars.
The tide comes in to spoil our fun,
But we're just grateful for the sun!

Shining Shores

On shiny shores, our fun begins,
We wear our floats like goofy fins.
A splash fight starts with giggles loud,
We're the mermaids of this sandy crowd.

Sun umbrellas like jellybeans,
We roast marshmallows, with funny scenes.
Stray dogs chase balls, oh what a sight,
Tangled in leashes, giving a fright.

Beach balls fly, they go astray,
Crashing into sunbathers' array.
We laugh and roll like tumbleweeds,
With laughter echoing across the reeds.

In our hats that are whimsically wide,
We pause to take a comical ride.
The sun dips low, our day has passed,
We'll remember these moments, forever cast.

Dances of Light and Waves

The water's shimmer is a playful friend,
Twirling with joy as we ascend.
Oceans clap, their frothy applause,
While flip-flops mysteriously pause!

Our shadows stretch, a dance in time,
In mismatched socks—we feel so prime.
Fish flip-flop, making us squeal,
We pretend we've started an ocean wheel.

A surfboard lost? Just take a ride,
On a giant wave of snack-attack pride.
With every splash, our worries flee,
Our laughter sails, wild and free.

The sunset's glow, like ketchup flies,
We giggle as the ketchup tries.
Tonight we'll feast, it's what we crave,
Tomorrow's tales are sure to wave!

Embracing the Dusk

As evening wraps with a vibrant hue,
We dance with shadows, just me and you.
With every twist, our feet do sway,
Like seaweed's ballet in a stylish way.

Fire pits glow, storytelling time,
With burnt marshmallows—a taste sublime.
The night plays tricks with shadows long,
In a chorus of laughter, our hearts belong.

As stars peek out, we start to jest,
Wishing the moon would join our fest.
The waves whisper secrets, oh what a sight,
Embracing dreams as we laugh into the night.

Riding the tides of twilight fun,
Wrapped in giggles as day is done.
With sand still clinging, we bid adieu,
To the playful moments, shared by two!

Whispers of the Azure Tides

There once was a fish who could sing,
He'd croon while he wore a gold ring.
With bubbles and glee,
So snazzy was he,
He danced in a seaweed swing.

The crabs clapped their claws in delight,
As starfish joined in for a fight.
They all tried to prance,
In a wobbly dance,
Oh what a comical sight!

A turtle appeared, slow and grand,
Claiming he was the best in the band.
But he tripped on a shell,
Fell right back, what the hell!
Now he sings with a flop while he's fanned.

So listen, my friends, to the cheer,
Of creatures who gather so near.
With laughter and song,
Where all do belong,
In waters of fun, never fear!

Sunlit Serenades on the Shore

A gull had a habit to squawk,
He'd steal all the food, what a shock!
With fries in his beak,
He'd strut like a freak,
As people would stare at his walk.

The sand crabs threw parties in pairs,
With hats that they made from old chairs.
They danced little jigs,
While pulling on twigs,
In seashells, their laughter declares.

A clam tried to serve up some drinks,
But spilled all the fizzy pinkinks.
The bubbles took flight,
What a colorful sight,
As everyone laughed until they blinked.

The sunset arrived like a star,
The ocean sang soft from afar.
With fun all around,
In joy we were bound,
Under the sky, how bizarre!

A Dance of Indigo and Gold

A dolphin once decided to bake,
He mixed with the seaweed and flake.
But oh what a mess,
He wore quite the dress,
With cake on his nose, what a quake!

The octopus played the guitar,
With eight arms, he'd strum from afar.
He sang in a pitch,
That made all the fish twitch,
As sea turtles cheered, 'You're a star!'

A shrimp joined in on the fun,
He'd hop around, never would run.
With a flip and a twirl,
He danced like a girl,
While everyone laughed till they spun.

So gather, dear friends in the tide,
Where joys of the ocean abide.
With giggles and splashes,
And no silly clashes,
In waters where laughter won't hide!

Radiant Reflections on Serene Waters

A whale with a hat made of foam,
Declared, 'This vast sea is my home!'
He'd wiggle and sway,
In a comical way,
While singing a tune all his own.

The jellyfish glowed like a light,
While dancing and prancing in flight.
They jiggled with glee,
Above the deep sea,
What a whimsical, wavy sight!

A sea cucumber told quite the tale,
Of pirates who'd sailed with a snail.
With treasure of gold,
And stories so bold,
He laughed as he rolled on the trail.

So join in the mirth of the sea,
Where all creatures live wild and free.
With jokes and with cheer,
Let's raise up a beer,
In waters of whimsy, you see!

Gold-tipped Waves

The sea reflects a shiny hue,
Like a fish wearing a golden shoe.
Surfboards wobble, people scream,
Trying hard to balance—what a dream!

Seagulls dive and steal a fry,
As they swoop and laugh, oh my!
Crabs on the beach have a dance so chic,
With sideways shuffles, a quirky peek.

Children splash with all their might,
Suddenly drenched, it's pure delight.
Sandcastles tumble in the breeze,
A sandy snack? Oh, if you please!

With shades on, everyone's a star,
Yelling, "Look, I can surf afar!"
But falling down is half the fun,
While chasing shadows of the sun.

Celestial Choreography

The jellyfish dance with floating grace,
In a wobbly waltz, they take their place.
Fish throw a party, oh what a sight,
With disco lights that spark in the night!

Turtles grooving in slow motion,
With a twist and twirl, in ocean's potion.
Every creature's got their groove,
As the tide sets in, they all improve.

Crabs don tiny hats—oh, how they prance,
While waves applaud this silly dance.
Underwater bubbles join the fun,
Making melodies till day is done.

Sharks try a cha-cha, but glide right past,
Keeping it suave, they're never last.
"Who knew the sea could be so grand?"
Giggles echo across the sand!

Liquid Gold

Sparkling surface, a dazzling show,
As if the sea got a treasure glow.
The surfers tumble, laughing galore,
Practicing stunts but crash on the shore!

Seashells hiding with secrets untold,
While crabs pull pranks—oh, they're so bold!
A splash of water, a twist of fate,
Not sure if it's fun or just too late!

The sun dips down like a buttered toast,
As we toast marshmallows, we love the most.
With sticky fingers and sandy feet,
We sing our songs to a rhythm sweet.

Every sunset is an artist's dream,
Painting the waves with a golden beam.
And when it's dark, the laughter stays,
Echoing softly through starry bays!

The Quiet Coast

On the quiet coast where giggles linger,
A dog gets splashed, what's with that finger?
People lounge like the world's a spa,
While seagulls plot mischief from afar.

Beach umbrellas like colorful mushrooms,
Dance in the wind—oh, such fun costumes!
Buckets filled with dreams and sand,
Where children pretend to be in command.

Flip-flops fly from toes in a race,
Caught in the tide with a splash, what a face!
The ice cream melts but joy remains,
As laughter rides the joyous waves.

Stars slowly peek from their hiding spots,
As evening settles, the mayhem softens.
But wait, there's a splash—what's that? Oh no!
Just a crab stealing a flip-flop show!

Solstice Serenade

The ocean laughs a quirky tune,
As seagulls dance beneath the moon.
Flip-flops flung like boomerangs,
Splashing friends, oh how it hangs!

A crab walks sideways with some sass,
He waves to folks who pass, alas!
Ice cream drips, a sticky fight,
Sticky fingers, what a sight!

Laughter mingles with the breeze,
Sunburned noses, silly knees.
A beach ball soars, we cheer and shout,
Who knew the sand could knock you out!

The sun dips low, the sky's aglow,
We dance like no one here can know.
Tangled hair and silly grins,
Another day where fun begins!

Celestial Veil

The clouds wear hats, quite bizarre,
While surfboards race like shooting stars.
A sunburned chap with shades so grand,
Claims he's the king of all the sand!

Tiny crabs throw parties at night,
Clinking shells, oh, what a sight!
And beach towels transform into capes,
All the kids make fun, no escapes!

A dolphin prances, quite the show,
I swear he winked, I promise, though!
With laughter echoing in the air,
Every wave is a joyful dare!

The sky blinks down, a cheeky wink,
As sunglasses slide, they slip and clink.
With ice-cold drinks, we toast the night,
To all the fun, our hearts take flight!

Tide's Embrace

The foamy crest sings songs of glee,
As beachgoers run wild, so free.
Sandwiches fly like a playful kite,
Watch out, my friend, hold on tight!

A crab in shades, swaying with flair,
Chasing folks here, there, everywhere.
With boogie boards and laughter loud,
The silly crew forms a big crowd!

A squirty toy gives quite a blast,
Soaking those who thought they'd last.
With giggles flying left and right,
It's pure chaos, what a delight!

A sunset serenade arrives,
As laughter echoes, and joy thrives.
And with the tide's sweet, playful tease,
We close the day, Oh, what a breeze!

Gilded Tranquility

The sun sits high, a molten ball,
While surfboards crash and people sprawl.
With grape-flavored ice in big ol' cups,
Summer fun just fills us up!

A sandcastle crowned with driftwood sticks,
As kids declare their ruling tricks.
"Behold our kingdom!" they boldly cry,
While the ocean giggles and waves goodbye!

With each splash, a melody plays,
As laughter drifts into the haze.
Seashells whisper secrets soft,
To every giggling kid aloft!

At day's end, the sky blushes gold,
With stories shared and laughter bold.
On this beach of joy and quest,
We find our peace, it's simply the best!

Shimmering Bliss

The ocean sang a silly tune,
Where seagulls pranced like little tykes,
In surfboards made of silver spoons,
They danced around like jumping bikes.

Jellyfish wore hats so grand,
As dolphins played their banjo strings,
They held a party on the sand,
And invited all the ocean kings.

Starfish did the twist and shout,
While crabs played tag without a care,
The tides would cheer, there was no doubt,
As seashells tried to braid their hair.

A mackerel took a selfie snap,
With waves that rolled in for a kiss,
While clam shells napped beneath the flap,
Such mirthful scenes, you wouldn't miss.

The Celestial Play

The sky wore shades of cotton candy,
While sunbeams tickled ocean's cheek,
A starfish stood, its stance quite dandy,
It dreamed of flying—not so bleak.

Uranus took a slide down Neptune,
In flip-flops bright, they caused a scene,
As every splash made laughter bloom,
Their shenanigans were quite the dream.

Octopuses juggled shiny rocks,
They're pros at entertaining crowds,
While turtles raced with funny socks,
No need for trophies, just their shrouds.

A crab recited poetry,
About the tides and flip-flop shoes,
As everyone laughed in harmony,
A cosmic play, with joyful hues.

Sun-drenched Reflections

In a tub of warm, bubbly fun,
The sun boasted with golden rays,
Rubber ducks danced, one by one,
As bubbles popped in comical ways.

The sea foam flipped like acrobats,
While mermaids attempted to bake,
With cakes that looked more like big hats,
And frosting that did giggles make.

Sandcastles wore glasses, so chic,
As crabs played chess on sandy shores,
With each roll of dice, they'd squeak,
And cheer for their winning scores.

A pelican cooked gourmet fries,
While fish debated what to wear,
In shimmery suits, the ocean flies,
Making waves and catching air.

Indigo Dreams

Under a blanket of twilight hues,
The moon made friends with plump sea toads,
They kicked back, sharing fishy news,
As laughter echoed down their roads.

A lobster painted with bright hues,
Held a brush like a crafty pro,
Creating art—so wildly infused,
The seashells giggled at the show.

Starfish seemed to forecast joy,
Predicting waves of happy thrills,
While sea cucumbers played with toys,
And did cartwheels on the hills.

Jellybeans drifted in the tide,
They'd chat about the latest trends,
As all around them smiles collide,
In nighttime fun that never ends.

Gilded Skies

When daybreak woke with gilded cheer,
The seagulls squawked a funny tune,
Waking fish with bubbles near,
Chicken-style, like they were marooned.

A little crab wore shades so bright,
While starfish played hopscotch in glee,
With each funny bump and slight,
They giggled through their jubilee.

A sea turtle showed off its dance,
With moves that made the dolphins laugh,
They took a break, just for a chance,
Then carved their names on algae's staff.

As twilight stole the day's delight,
The waves did wink and gently sway,
"Oh what a sight!" they'd sing at night,
In ocean fun, they'd play away.

The Tranquil Expanse

In a sea of laughter, fish do sway,
They giggle and wiggle, in their own way.
Seagulls squawk jokes, perched in their glee,
While crabs do the cha-cha, as happy as can be.

A dolphin shows off, flips in a swirl,
Says, "Look at me, I'm a sea pearls' girl!"
The tide brings in stories, salty and bright,
As shells whisper secrets beneath the moonlight.

Frogs by the shore sing a silly tune,
Hopping in time, a croaking cartoon.
The breeze tickles sandcastles, makes them shake,
As children burst into giggles, for fun's sake.

So come join the party, bring your best hat,
With laughter like sunshine, imagine that!
In this jolly playground where all creatures play,
We'll dance with the dolphins, till the end of the day.

Waves of Morning Light

A turtle in sunglasses, looking quite cool,
Says, "Time to relax, and just play the fool!"
Fish toss a beach ball with scales all aglow,
While jellyfish glide by, putting on a show.

The sun peeks in, with a wink and a grin,
"Get up, you lazy waves, let the fun begin!"
With bubbles as hats, they splash about,
Tickling the toes of all who stand out.

A crab in a hammock, swaying with ease,
Sipping on seaweed smoothies, oh, what a breeze!
The shells all applaud, they rock back and forth,
As laughter erupts from the sea's gentle north.

No need to worry, just let spirits soar,
With each wave that dances, there's always more.
So let's ride the surf, let's jump and we'll cheer,
The ocean is calling, let's spread the good cheer!

Luminous Ocean Serenade

A clam sings sweet tunes, its pearls shining bright,
While starfish tap dance under the soft light.
Octopuses juggle, oh what a sight,
As crabs clap along, bringing joy and delight.

"Hey there, you fish, come join in the fun!"
Yells the moon from above, just as golden days run.
With bubbles to pop and currents that play,
It's a watery concert to brighten the day.

A boat with a parrot squawking loud pranks,
Pirouettes on the waves, while everyone thanks.
"That's one silly bird, with a beak so grand!"
As laughter rolls over the picturesque sand.

With rhythm and laughter, the sea seems alive,
In bubbles of joy, we'll dive and we'll thrive.
So gather your friends, let's dance through the tide,
With the ocean serenade, let happiness ride!

Hues of Dawn's Awakening

The sky brushes colors, bright and absurd,
As dolphins put on shows, it's all quite stirred.
The tides tickle toes, with giggles galore,
While little fish prank, sending waves to the shore.

A starfish in flip-flops, shuffles with flair,
Claims, "I've got moves, watch me dance if you dare!"
With rays that bring laughter, the day starts anew,
As waves whisper secrets, "We're happy with you!"

Seagulls trade jokes, goofing off like a band,
Their feathers all fluffing, together they stand.
The sun yells, "Rise up! The fun will not end!"
In this playful realm, where even shells blend.

So let's splash and rumble, let's savor the mirth,
For each laugh that rises brings joy to the earth.
With every hue shining, let's cheer with delight,
For life's a great party, from morn until night!

Dance of the Seafoam

The foam does a jig on the shore,
It sloshes and splashes, then begs for more.
Sandcastles quiver, afraid of the wave,
While seagulls laugh, feeling quite brave.

Crabs holding hands in a wobbly line,
Shuffling along, thinking they're fine.
The seaweed sways, it's quite the sight,
Dancing so well, it lifts the night.

A beach ball bounces, with great delight,
Chasing the children, oh what a fright!
The tide pulls back, steals their flip-flops,
The giggles erupt as the fun never stops.

So here we are, on this sandy spree,
With laughter that bubbles, joyfully free.
The ocean's a stage, where all play their part,
In costumes of foam, we dance with our heart.

Sun-kissed Tides

A lobster sings as he struts on the sand,
While starfish chuckle, forming a band.
The sun winks down with a mischievous glare,
As seashells gossip, without any care.

Surfboards crash, with a splash and a flair,
Fishermen giggle at the seagull's despair.
A dolphin does flips, showcasing its style,
While kiddos all cheer, it's been quite a while!

The old man by the pier throws bread with great pride,
While pigeons and gulls gather on the side.
A sprinkle of sea holds the laughter so light,
As waves break again, reflecting sheer delight.

In the sun's warm embrace, we frolic and play,
With the tide's gentle pull, we'll never stray.
So let's soak it in, in our sun-kissed domain,
Where each wave that rolls up sings a joyous refrain.

Whispering Waters

The ocean whispers secrets to sand,
As splashes of laughter fill up the land.
Shells tell the tales, of pirate ships bold,
While baby crabs dance, never feeling old.

Gulls dive around, with their silly caws,
Chasing the snacks, they flaunt their claws.
The breeze plays a tune, through palm trees it sighs,
As it tickles the waves, like a friendly surprise.

Kite-flying kids giggle, the strings in a tangle,
Their laughter erupts, a delightful jangle.
A surf rat slips, in a quick flight,
As all of the beach gives a shrill, shared delight.

The waning sun paints the sky all aglow,
With hues of a party, oh what a show!
As the day whispers softly its sweet goodbye,
We promise to return, oh my, oh my!

The Golden Embrace

Sunset's ribbons stretch across the sea,
While fish throw a party, as bold as can be.
With finned friends dancing, they twirl in delight,
The shimmer of scales sparkles in the light.

Tiny umbrellas peek from cool, shady spots,
As parents sip drinks, forgetting their knots.
Bikini-clad heroes dive without fear,
While beach balls bounce as the laughter draws near.

The sand takes its toll with each giggle and scream,
As friends build some castles, a whimsical dream.
A rubber duck races, with confidence laid,
While someone yells out, "Is that a mermaid?"

As shadows grow long and the stars start to gleam,
The evening unfolds like a fantastic dream.
With laughter and warmth in this golden embrace,
We revel in memories, this sweet, happy place.

Celestial Surf

The sky's a big jelly, all wobbly and round,
With a splashy old seal who just wouldn't sit down.
He grooves on the seaweed, does the twist and twirl,
While flip-flops wash out to join in the whirl.

Seagulls play tag with some chips from a snack,
Chasing each other, they form quite a pack.
One steals a sandwich, oh what a delight!
While the sun's on a diet, it's glowing so bright.

The ocean's a canvas, where surfers do paint,
With splashes of laughter, pure joy they create.
They tumble and fumble, all dressed in their gear,
As the waves give a wink, "Come join in the cheer!"

As everyone spills from their beach chairs with glee,
A tumble of sand ends up covering me.
"Who knew a sunbathe could be such a mess?"
But hey, if you're laughing, it's truly a success!

Shimmers of Light

The sun plays peekaboo, it blinks on the sea,
While dolphins do flips, giggling, 'Look at me!'
There's a crab wearing shades, with swagger so grand,
He struts on the shoreline as if he's the man.

A clam throws a party, it's all quite absurd,
With shrimp in a conga line, haven't you heard?
They dance on the sand, with shells in a spin,
Laughing so loudly, "Come join in our win!"

There's a bucket of dreams that a child just filled,
With castles and moats, and they almost got grilled.
But look! An old seagull swoops down with a shout,
"Hey kid, I could use a snack, mind if I pout?"

The waves start to giggle, they jiggle and swell,
As sunblocky penguins try surfing quite well.
They crash and they laugh, it's a feathery ball,
The sight brings a smile that just can't help but sprawl.

Harmony of the Horizon

The horizon's a playground, where colors collide,
As the sun throws a party with friends by its side.
A jellyfish juggles, with a wink and a smile,
While the sandcastles cheer, "Let's stay here a while!"

Surfboards on standby, like soldiers at ease,
While crabs in tuxedos come out to appease.
They wave tiny flags, their antics so grand,
"This beach needs a DJ, won't you lend us a hand?"

The pelican slides in, with style and grace,
Saying, "I'm here for the fun, just look at my face!"
He brings out some snacks, like fish sticks and chips,
While everyone laughs at his clumsy flip-flips.

With shells as their stage, and the sun as their light,
They dance through the day, oh what a delight!
The ocean applauds with each splash and each wave,
In this goofy old paradise, everyone's brave!

The Misty Calm

A foggy old morning, the laughter's on hold,
While clams in their shells tell stories of old.
They whisper of mermaids, who come for a glance,
But they only find fishermen, lost in their trance.

The seaweed looks silly, all tangled and free,
It trips up a turtle who giggles with glee.
"Watch where you're going!" cries a gull with a frown,
As the surf rolls in, it's a watery clown.

The sun peeks with mischief, to lighten the mist,
While fish start a game of "Don't get kissed!"
The crabs throw their claws up, in a dance so absurd,
As the waves join in laughter; oh, what's that you heard?

A party of seagulls now hovers above,
Screaming "Join us in fun, you'll fall in love!"
And in this calm chaos, they bubble and teem,
As we skip through this day, lost in a dreamy beam!

The Ocean's Lullaby

A fish in a suit, he dived with grace,
Flipping his tail, what a funny face!
Seagulls cawed tunes with a witty sway,
While crabs danced the cha-cha at the break of day.

A dolphin did juggle with seashells galore,
He slipped on a starfish and rolled on the shore.
The tide tickled toes, a soft, gentle tease,
As everyone laughed with the whoosh of the breeze.

Shells whispered secrets, oh what a sight,
A clam in a top hat felt quite polite.
With barnacles glued, he stood up so proud,
While the tide splashed on, drawing a giggling crowd.

So under the rays, where the wild things roam,
The ocean sang softly, calling us home.
With waves full of laughter, we jumped in delight,
In a sea of shenanigans, everything's right!

Dawn's Embrace, Tidal Dreams beneath a Gilded Sky

The morning arrived with a splash and a spin,
A seal wore a hat, showing off with a grin.
Bright rays bounced brightly, painting the sea,
While octopuses danced, quite comically free.

The shoreline was busy, all creatures around,
A crab played the tambourine, lost in the sound.
Starfish applauded, they clapped with their arms,
As the surf merged and mingled with its silly charms.

A pelican plotted to steal a quick snack,
But a wave stole his sandwich, oh what a whack!
With laughter and shrieks as the gulls took their flight,
The dawn breathed a giggle, all things felt so right.

So let the tide carry our worries away,
With each splash of water, let's dance and play.
For tomorrow will come with its own sunny glee,
But let's live for today, wild and carefree!

Chasing Horizons in Sapphire Light

A turtle named Ted raced to catch a quick wave,
With flip-flops on fins, oh what a brave knave!
He winked at the whales, who just rolled their big eyes,
While dolphins spun circles, plotting surfboards' surprise.

The sun wore a grin as it peeped through the mist,
"Last one to the reef is a fish on a list!"
With splashes and bubbles, they sped down the blue,
Creating a ruckus in the wet morning dew.

A shark tried a somersault, failed with a flop,
As octopuses giggled, they couldn't quite stop.
With laughter erupting from the deep ocean floor,
Each creature became part of the great sea encore.

So here's to adventures that make our hearts race,
With jellyfish gliding, they're lighting the place.
We'll chase all horizons, oh what a delight,
In this wondrous world that feels oh-so right!

Sun-Kissed Ripples of Tranquil Delight

The tide turned and twisted, a dance of pure fun,
With each playful wave, we'd laugh in the sun.
A pelican juggled, with fish to impress,
While sandcastles crumbled in a comical mess.

The sunbeams laughed too, in a playful embrace,
As we splattered and splashed through this watery place.
A turtle named Harriet wore shades like a star,
Said, "Life is a beach, and I'm driving the car!"

See seahorses spinning in foam-topped delight,
And seals that are twirling like tipsy kite flight.
The laughter erupted, echoing loud,
As jellyfish chuckled, amusing the crowd.

So, here in this haven where giggles run free,
We'll dance with the tides, just you wait and see.
With sun-kissed ripples and hearts oh-so light,
Let's savor the laughter until comes the night!

www.ingramcontent.com/pod-product-compliance
Lightning Source LLC
Chambersburg PA
CBHW050317100526
44585CB00016BA/1495